Do You Have Paper?

Seed Learning

paper

glue

brush

paint

card

pencils

pens

crayons

Do you
have paper?

Yes, I do.

Do you
have crayons?

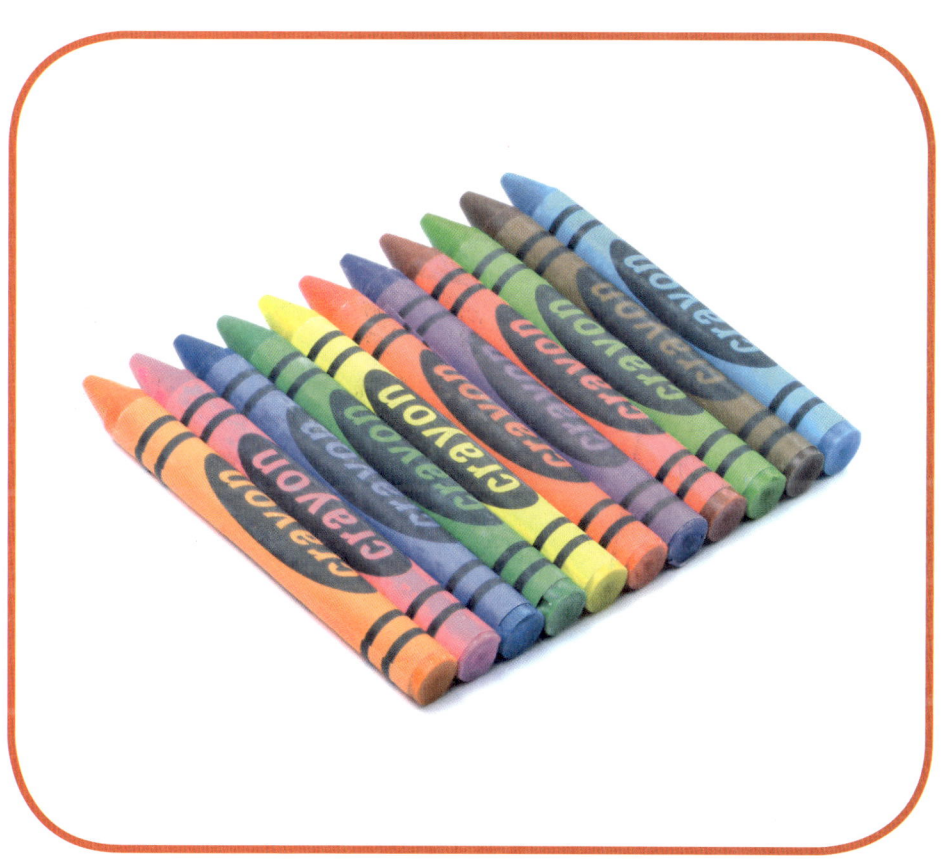

Yes, I do.

Do you
have paint?

Yes, I do.

Do you
have a brush?

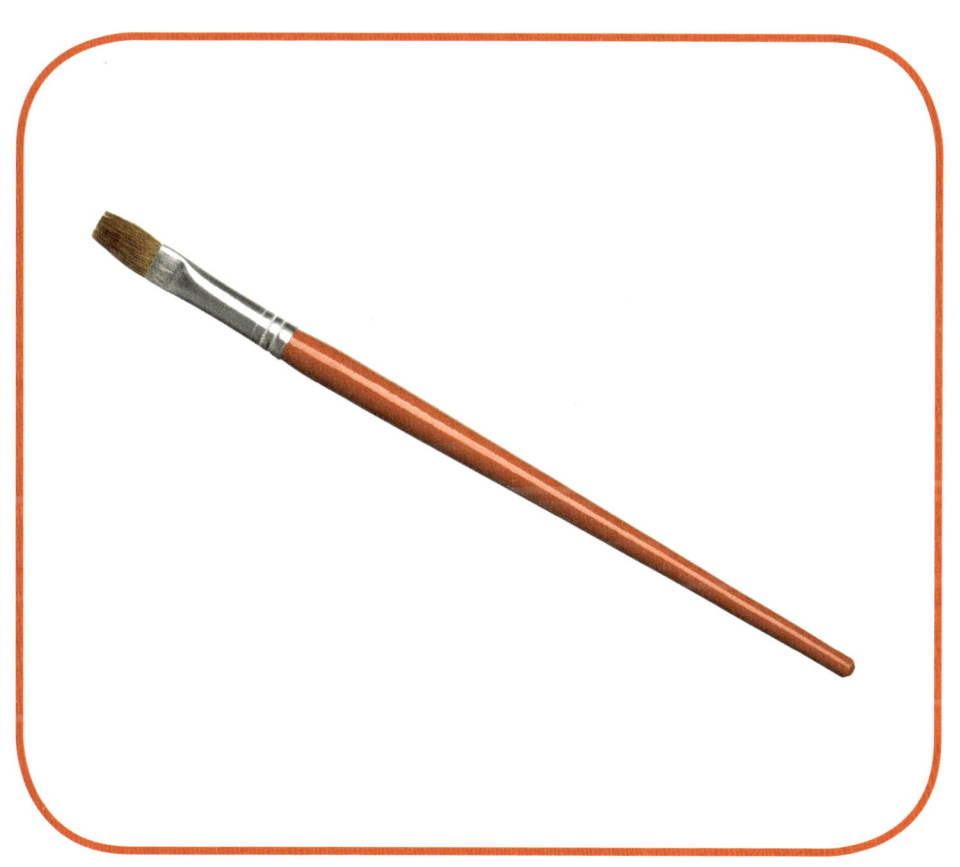

Yes, I do.

Do you
have glue?

Yes, I do.

Do you
have a card?

Yes, I do.

Let's learn more about Canada.

Maple syrup